Photographs for the Tsar

Photographs for the Tsar

The pioneering color photography of
Sergei Mikhailovich Prokudin-Gorskii
commissioned by Tsar Nicholas II

Edited, with an introduction by Robert H. Allshouse

The Dial Press ❦ New York

Published by The Dial Press
1 Dag Hammarskjold Plaza
New York, New York 10017

Manufactured in the United States of America

Second printing 1981

Printed in the United States of America by A. Hoen & Co.
Photographic development and separations by A. Hoen & Co. and
Lincoln Lithoplate.
Design by Jack Ribik
Production by Warren Wallerstein

Library of Congress Cataloging in Publication Data

Prokudin-Gorskii, S. M.
Photographs for the Tsar.

1. Prokudin-Gorskii, S. M.
2. Photography, Artistic.
3. Russia—Description and
travel—Views.
4. Photographers—Russia—Biography.
I Allshouse, Robert H.
II Title.
TR140.P76A34   779′.9947083   80-17056
ISBN: 0-8037-6996-2

For Lisa, Heather, and Todd
and especially Marcia

ACKNOWLEDGMENTS

This work would not have been possible without the help of Gannon University, which provided the initial funding for this journey in the form of a Faculty Senate Award. To Dr. Joseph P. Scottino, President of the University, and to Dr. Frank F. Angotti and Dr. Matti Moosa of the Department of History I owe a debt of thanks for reading portions of my proposals and manuscript material and making valuable criticisms and suggestions.

The main source of the photographic material was the Library of Congress. The author is indebted to those individuals at the Library who gave freely of their time to make this project viable. Dr. Alan Fern, Director of Special Collections, was most helpful in untangling the complicated technical and logistical problems. Dudley Ball, Jerry Kearns, and Jerry Maddox of the Prints and Photographs Division extended every courtesy in the Reading Room, and Carolyn Sung and Buddy King from the Photo-duplication Division were very helpful in expediting the necessary materials. A special accolade is due Elisabeth W. Betz, Picture Cataloging Specialist in the Prints and Photographs Division, who was unflagging in her efforts at locating, labeling, and identifying glass plates that had hitherto proved elusive.

The author owes a special debt to the photographer's family for their help. Through the efforts of Mrs. Edward Petersen the author was able to contact S.M. Prokudin-Gorskii's daughter, Madame Hélène Soussaline, and her son, Dr. Michel Soussaline. Their kindness in submitting to transatlantic telephone interviews was exceeded only by their generosity in meeting requests for Prokudin-Gorskii's notebooks, manuscripts, and pictures. Additional material was received from the Royal Photographic Society of Great Britain. The staff very kindly provided aid in locating Prokudin-Gorskii's writings while in the midst of moving to new quarters.

Thanks are owed to Dr. Joseph W. Ink, Dr. Borys Bilokur, R. Mark Gajdos, and Rev. Steven Simon for providing resource material at the spur of the moment; to Joseph Dascanio and Mr. and Mrs. Lauren Hart for their hospitality; to Lisa Allshouse for several translations; and to Mortimer Graves, whose interest in this project was matched only by his zeal in promoting the use of the Prokudin-Gorskii collection. Special thanks for their invaluable help with translation must go to Maria F. Komarow and to Mr. and Mrs. Vladimir J. Archipow.

Juris Jurjevics and Warren Wallerstein of The Dial Press gave whole-hearted and enthusiastic approval to the project; Jack Ribik, Francesca Belanger, and Doris Sullivan reinforced the author's efforts with their own capable work. Joyce Johnson's probing insight and ever-sharp editorial pencil gave shape and dimension to the manuscript. Any errors or omissions are, of course, the responsibility of the author.

Contents

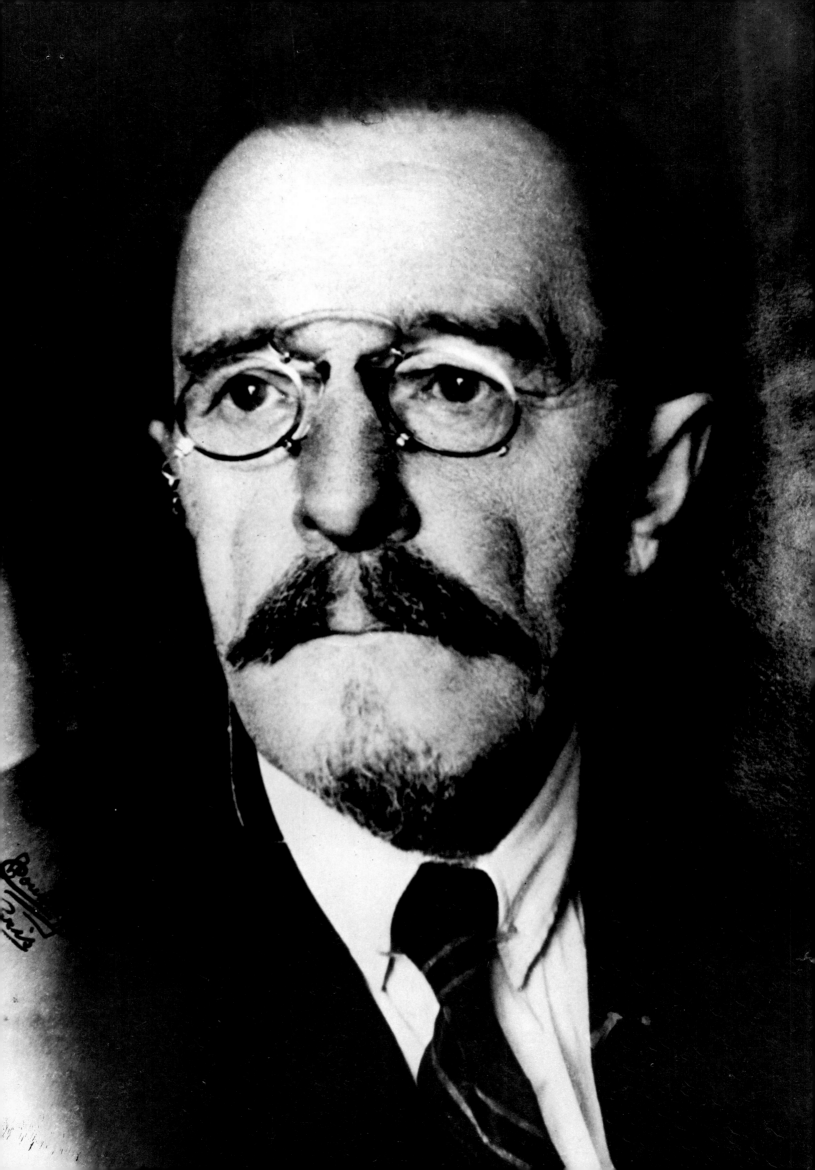

Introduction

This collection of photos of Imperial Russia prior to World War I, taken by a single photographer, is an historical journey of unusual dimensions—a trip in a time machine to a past rendered in color. We are so accustomed to seeing pictures of this era in sepia tones that the experience of viewing Prokudin-Gorskii's work is almost one of cultural shock. Yet here is what has disappeared forever—eradicated by the relentless forces of war, revolution, and time—looking as though it were captured by the photographer only yesterday.

Sergei Mikhailovich Prokudin-Gorskii was a chemist as well as a photographer and artist, and was one of the pioneers in developing an advanced process for taking colored pictures. His name appears in none of our contemporary histories of photography, however. Like Imperial Russian society, he too was a victim of the upheaval of the Revolution. In 1918 he became one of the countless émigrés forced to flee Russia. Eminent as a photographer in his own country, he disappeared into relative obscurity in Norway, England, and France—although he still continued to pursue his researches into the development of color, in cinematography as well as in photography.

Having lost all his money and property, Prokudin-Gorskii went into exile, taking with him only his collection of nearly 2,000 glass-plate negatives and his photograph albums. Much of this work dated from the years 1909–15, when, under commission from Tsar Nicholas II, Prokudin-Gorskii traveled throughout the vast reaches of the Russian Empire photographing "things of interest and significance" in what he called "natural color." Prokudin-Gorskii had hoped the glass plates would eventually be projected on screens in schoolrooms for the instruction of Russian youth. Till the end of his life he believed passionately in the educative function of photography: "Photography," he wrote, "penetrates into all domains of knowledge... Memory, aided visually by an interesting[ly] exhibited subject, will leave our ordinary methods of memorizing far behind." In Nice, where he lived in the 1920s, he gave slide shows for the émigré community so that "young Russians who had been so long in exile and in foreign schools" would have a way to remember their heritage. He hoped his pictures would serve "as a document as to what their homeland was in reality."

"The eye," he wrote, "sensates...nature and not a picture." Color photography was infinitely superior to monochromatic photography because:

Ordinary photography is especially helpless in the reproduction of the vegetative world, in geology, ethnography, etc. It reproduces the shapes of the objects, and not the contents...

Therefore, one could only conclude that "photography in natural color is the best way to teach and to provide an example."

Sergei Mikhailovich Prokudin-Gorskii was born in St. Petersburg in 1863.

It is said that he was descended from one of the oldest noble families in the province of Vladimir. In St. Petersburg he received his early education at the Imperial Alexander Lyceum and then matriculated in the Faculty of Natural Sciences at the Institute of Applied Technology. His leanings were artistic as well as scientific. For a while he apparently had ambitions to be a violinist, but during his student days his left hand was severely injured in a laboratory accident, and for the next few years he pursued his studies in chemistry in a single-minded way. Perhaps he was inspired by the example of his teacher, the brilliant chemist D. I. Mendeleev, best known to us for his periodic table of elements. In 1922, in his autobiographical notes, he remembered his studies with Mendeleev with pride, recalling how in 1887, at the age of fifty-three, the professor had taken a solo balloon flight to observe the solar eclipse—demonstrating in one action the exploratory nature of science while pointing out the yet uncharted vistas of the scientific frontier.

Having been initiated into the rigors of research, with training in viscosity, thermal expansion, capillary action of fluids, metrology, and meteorology, Prokudin-Gorskii left the Institute in 1889, when he was twenty-six years old, and went abroad. For a time he was a chemistry instructor at the High Technical School in Charlottenburg, where he lectured on spectral analysis and photochemistry. It was while he was in Germany that he became interested in studying the problems of color photography scientifically and came into contact with Adolph Mieth, who had taken the chair of chemistry vacated by Dr. Hermann Wilhelm Vogel, a pioneer in orthochromatism ("correct color"), at the Technische Hochschule in Berlin. In 1903 Mieth was to extend the sensitivity of Vogel's orthochromatic plates from blue to yellow and red, an important step toward making panchromatic emulsions reproducing all colors.

Moving on to Paris, Prokudin-Gorskii continued his studies in the laboratory of the noted chemist Edmé Jules Maumené, who was doing research on color photography. In 1893 Maumené published a work on the subject, *Manuel de chimie photographique.*

By then Prokudin-Gorskii had returned to Russia, where he plunged into his chosen field with vigor. He quickly became a member of the Russian Imperial Technological Society and by 1897 had developed a series of courses for training individuals in photography and phototechnical studies, the first such establishment in the country. Among his students were a number of physicians who came to study microphotography, including Dr. D. K. Zabolotnyi, one of the leading figures of his day in microbiology and epidemiology.

His workshops proved successful, and soon Prokudin-Gorskii was able to expand his activities to include publication—at his own expense—of several books: *O pechatanii (kopirovanii) s' negativov'* (On Printing—Copying—with Negatives) and *O fotografirovanii momental'nimi ruchnimi kamerami* (Instant Photographing with Hand Cameras). With the outbreak of the Russo-Japanese War (1904), he journeyed to Korea and took a series of black-and-white photographs, which he published as a military yearbook. The sales from these works proved financially rewarding.

It was after 1904 that he began to work on the development of color-sensitive photographic plates. Within a year he had perfected a new method that gave equal sensitivity throughout the spectrum, and he began to take color pictures of natural scenes suitable for projection. In 1905 he gave the first report of his work at the general meeting of the Photographic Section of the Russian Imperial Technological Society.

The enthusiasm that greeted this report led to an invitation to repeat the lecture at the public meeting of the General Assembly, as well as to Prokudin-Gorskii's election as chairman of the Photographic Section and an honorary membership in the Russian Imperial Photographic Society. Memberships in the Photographic Society of Moscow and the St. Petersburg Photographic Society were soon to follow—the latter of particular consequence because the honorary chairman was the Grand Duke Mikhail Aleksandrovich, brother of Emperor Nicholas II.

In 1906, Prokudin-Gorskii took over the editorship of *Fotograf-Liubitel'* (Amateur Photographer), a Russian monthly photographic magazine. His predecessor, A. M. Lavrov, had founded the magazine some sixteen years earlier, and had been looking for a qualified successor for some time. In the November 1905 issue Lavrov stated that he had finally found the right person. "Sergei Mikhailovich Prokudin-Gorskii was not self-educated," like so many photographers, but was a chemist of some standing. Many individuals had been impressed by the exhibitions he had given in Moscow and St. Petersburg. It was noted that Prokudin-Gorskii's training had included a period of study under the German chemist Mieth, and in the editor's opinion he "had gone further than his teacher."

In his opening editorial Prokudin-Gorskii thanked Lavrov for the kind words, but reminded his readers that the quality of the magazine was due to Lavrov's selfless dedication. Lavrov "had taken a big step forward," and if he had been concerned "only with making money," the magazine would not hold its present position. Prokudin-Gorskii then pledged himself to uphold Lavrov's high standards.

Photography for Prokudin-Gorskii was a profession, one that demanded the proper scientific background and training. Yet he felt strongly the prospects for photography were so exciting that it should not remain in the exclusive domain of the technical experts. Assessing the transformation of photography as a result of the changeover from the wet-collodion process to the dry process in one of his editorials, he stated that "from the artistic point of view photography began to lose, but gained considerably in another—maybe more valuable—respect, namely, that of being spread among the masses."

During the four years of Prokudin-Gorskii's editorship, *Fotograf-Liubitel'* became a vehicle for his views. His philosophy of life, his sense of purpose,

his professional commitment to science, and his artistry all spring from the pages of the journal.

One of his editorials was written in Turkestan, as Prokudin-Gorskii was preparing to view an eclipse of the sun (January 4, 1907) from the Tian-Shania Mountains. He noted that the next solor eclipse would be visible in St. Petersburg and the surrounding areas. Russian photographers should be giving serious thought to preparing for it, he declared. If the equipment was not adequate—as some Russian photographers claimed— then they "should invent those things that are necessary" to carry out the project. "There are too many of us who say it cannot be done." If "only ten percent of Russian photographers were to work on this project, it would be a very big accomplishment." He believed that Russian techniques were at a level to sustain any such effort, and that his countrymen had the capability to accomplish even very complicated and difficult tasks in photography. But, he admonished them, "we [must] know how to put these goals ahead of us."

In a like manner he refused to subscribe to the belief that Russian photographic techniques were in any way inferior to those of other European nations. The best of the Russian work could compete on equal terms with any entries from abroad. While it was true that Russians were at a disadvantage because of tariffs and legislation, the simple fact remained that Russia had some of the best scientific minds in the world, and their accomplishments were in every way equal to those of other Europeans. "In the west, they don't want anything to do [with Russians]," because they were "afraid of competition."

He cited a personal example. In recent years he had attempted to duplicate a series of experiments in color photography written up in one of the Western journals. He had been unable to get the desired results, however, even though he went according to the formulas. When he inquired of his European colleagues as to how they were proceeding, they all answered that "they got good results" using the same method. Still unable to get the proper chemical reaction, Prokudin-Gorskii conducted a further series of experiments in that process. By modifying the procedure, he was able to get good results, "better than [his] neighbors." In talking with them afterward, he "understood from their faces and their speech that they were doing the same thing and achieving the same results." This incident—according to Prokudin-Gorskii—was only one of many that provided proof of Russian capabilities.

By 1904 Prokudin-Gorskii had also envisioned his grand educative scheme of photographing all of the Russian Empire in color—its varied peoples and natural beauties, its monuments, historic buildings and places. But such a plan required expenditures "which no one person could afford." For one thing there were vast distances to traverse. It would be necessary to travel by rail, ship, automobile, and wagon. Special equipment would also have to be obtained from Europe.

Securing official help would be a slow and tedious process, filled with delays and with no guarantee of success. However, he was up to the task at hand. Now that he had solved his technical problems, it would be less of a challenge to overcome the inertia of the bureaucracy.

He had, in fact, developed a system of producing three-part color photographs that could be projected simultaneously. Using a small folding hand camera of the type designed by Mieth, he photographed three exposures of the same subject, made at about one-second intervals on a glass plate approximately 84–88 mm wide and 232 mm long, which was mounted vertically in the camera. The plate dropped to a new position after each exposure, and the image was captured through three different color-separation filters. Because of the need to take the same picture three times, Prokudin-Gorskii was limited to subjects that would make no movement. Thus, much of what he recorded consisted of fixed objects.*

*Publisher's Note: Although great efforts were made to reproduce these remarkable photographs at the highest quality levels possible, there are imperfections visible in places. Time has taken its inevitable toll of some of the fragile glass photographic plates, causing flaws in prints. Also, the primitive techniques employed occasionally caused blurring in the original plates. Because of overriding historical interest, such factors were overlooked several times during the selection process.

Above left: Viewing the solar eclipse
Below: Prokudin-Gorskii with two soldiers
Right: Boat supplied by Ministry of Ways and Communications

He had also developed a special treatment that hypersensitized the Ilford "red label" plates he was using. After developing, the images could easily supply contact prints, from which excellent color photographs could be made. The remaining problem lay with overcoming the difficulties that arose when the standard projection systems were used in conjunction with his three-part separations.

His unique solution was a projector first developed by F. E. Ives, which he modified so that "from the point of view of rapidity of arrangements and quality it gave better results…" He had it constructed in Germany to his specifications, using three rhomboidal prisms cemented together to make one combination prism. By adjusting the focal lengths and correcting for distortion so that the optical distances became equal, he was able to focus the three colors on the screen precisely.

In typical fashion Prokudin-Gorskii began his campaign for government approval scientifically, conducting a public opinion poll of influential people in St. Petersburg, to ascertain just which photographic subject matter would attract the most interest to his project, particularly that of the Tsar. Then he proceeded to take the pictures that would help him win his case.

But there were still major political problems involved. The Tsar and his supporting bureaucracy kept portions of Russia closed off even to its own citizens. Permits would be necessary to gain access to the transportation networks. In addition the taking of pictures was officially prohibited in many areas, and thus much of what Prokudin-Gorskii wanted to capture on film would be off limits. What particularly worried him was the all-pervasive network of police spies who saw to it that these restrictions were enforced.

The sheer scope and magnitude of the project was mind-boggling, and it began to take on the aura of a dream. It would have remained so, had not fate—in the person of the Grand Duke Mikhail Aleksandrovich—intervened. The Grand Duke was interested in color photography, and in his position as honorary chairman of the St. Petersburg Photographic Society had helped to foster a public interest in this medium. He was familiar with the photographs Prokudin-Gorskii had taken of Tolstoy at Yasnaya Polyana in 1908, as well as his reports to the Society and his work on *Fotograf-Liubitel'*. After viewing Prokudin-Gorskii's public demonstrations the Grand Duke invited him to give a private showing at his residence. The success of this show led to another invitation, this one from the Dowager Empress Maria Fedorovna, widow of Alexander III and mother of the Tsar.

Prokudin-Gorskii was well aware that this demonstration would have to be apolitical. He would appeal to the universal element of love of nature and rely on the breathtaking beauty of pictures in color. He would, in addition, have to tailor his individual presentations to his aristocratic audience. His years of teaching and his scientific background gave him that ability.

The presentation at Gatchina, the 900-room Imperial palace erected by Catherine the Great, lived up to the expectations not only of the Grand Duke, but of Count P. K. Benckendorff, a longtime member of the Court, who had a great deal of influence. Benckendorff had risen to Adjutant-General and Grand Marshal of the Court under Nicholas II and was a man whose carefully chosen words were heeded. Within a short period of time Prokudin-Gorskii received an invitation to present his pictures to the Tsar and the Imperial Court at Tsarskoe Selo.

The symbolic representation of the heritage and grandeur of the Romanov autocracy, Tsarskoe Selo was a place of legend and enchantment. In his book *The Real Romanovs*, Gleb Botkin, the son of Nicholas II's court physician, wrote: "Tsarskoe Selo was a world apart, an enchanted fairyland to which only a small number of people had the right of entry." These chosen few now included Prokudin-Gorskii.

A special train was sent to the Vitebsk Railway Station in St. Petersburg the day of his appearance before the Tsar during the winter of 1909. Prokudin-Gorskii and his assistants loaded their equipment upon it and made the fifteen-mile journey south from the capital. Upon their early morning arrival they were met at their destination and driven down the wide boulevard that connected the small provincial railway with the gates of the Imperial Park.

Special rooms on the second floor had been set aside for them in the state apartments in the center section of the Alexander Palace. Inhabiting the two wings on either side of Prokudin-Gorskii's apartment were the Court ministers, along with those in service to the members of the royal family, and the royal family itself. At eleven in the morning, after they had been served a specially prepared breakfast in their rooms, Prokudin-Gorskii and his assistants began to set up the apparatus in the Palace auditorium. They took time out for dinner, and by six o'clock everything was in readiness. A large white projection screen had been hung over the stage masked by rich black velvet curtains.

Shortly before eight thirty the Grand Dukes and Grand Duchesses, the ministers of the Court, the ladies- and gentlemen-in-waiting, and specially invited guests took their seats. Then an anticipatory hush settled over the crowd. To Prokudin-Gorskii's right was the door through which the Emperor of All the Russias would enter. The photographer knew that it was too late to make any changes: "Here was the moment upon which all my work depended. It was the first time the Tsar would see slides projected in natural colors."

He had chosen his slides very carefully: pictures of flowers, which would have special appeal for the Empress Alexandra; autumn landscapes having a universal beauty that even the dullest bureaucrat could comprehend; scenes of devoutly religious peasants, overwhelmingly loyal to the *Batush-ka* and *Matushka*; and pictures of children—the wellspring of Russia's future greatness.

At precisely eight thirty the page on duty announced, "His Majesty, the Emperor." The doors silently swung open and through the doorway came the Tsar, escorting the Tsaritsa and accompanied by the Romanov children. The Tsar shook hands with Prokudin-Gorskii, and the royal family took their seats. Nicholas then asked him to begin. The lights dimmed, then darkened completely. The black velvet draperies, powered by remote-controlled electric motors, glided noiselessly aside. Just as the viewers had accustomed their eyes to the darkness, Prokudin-Gorskii gave the signal to the projection booth, and the projector was switched on. The screen filled with a breathtaking image of birches in "natural color." "From this small ray of light," he later wrote, "there were beautiful pictures."

During the first portion of the show Prokudin-Gorskii heard the whispers of the royal family, and felt "rather certain that [he] was successful." At intermission tea and soft drinks were served. The Tsar left the group he was with, and came to talk with the photographer. "What do you have in mind for this beautiful work?" the Tsar asked. "What is the future for your apparatus and pictures such as these?" Finally Prokudin-Gorskii had the undivided attention of Nicholas, with no one to interrupt him or change the thrust of the conversation, but his time was limited. He had to distill his thoughts into just a few sentences. The future, he replied, was in education. He envisioned the use of projectors of this type in schools all across the Russian Empire. "They would show students in every school the grandeur of Holy Mother Russia." The heritage of Russia was richly represented in the churches and monasteries—and their important and revered ikons—as well as the historical monuments that recorded events of national consequence. The centennial year of Napoleon's defeat was just several years away. All of these things should be part of the historical consciousness of His Majesty's subjects, so that "they might better appreciate the heritage of their glorious motherland." Given the needs of the state, he added, "it might also prove interesting for His Imperial Majesty to see such pictures from time to time." The Tsar was very pleased.

Nicholas II then told Prokudin-Gorskii to contact S. V. Rukhlov, the Minister of Ways and Communication, and to give him a list of the specifics needed for a project of this nature. It should be, of course, as complete and as comprehensive as possible. Rukhlov would then report to the Tsar as to the status of the project. Prokudin-Gorskii assured the Tsar that he would do just that. Then the Tsar returned to his seat and the intermission was over.

Nicholas II was so noted for his extraordinary politeness and unfailing courtesy that Prokudin-Gorskii must have had some doubt about his real enthusiasm. Many a minister had thought that the ideas he had just put forth were received favorably by the sovereign,only to find a request for his resignation on his desk the following day. It is possible that Nicholas was reacting merely to the novelty of the presentation, since he had never seen slides in natural color before that evening's showing at the palace.

As Prokudin-Gorskii began the second half of the program, his entrepreneurial instincts took over. Now there would be more drama and excitement—he had made sure of that. In addition he had carefully tailored his narrative to the projected images. His confidence continued to build as the pictures flashing on the screen created a stirring in the audience. "The whispers had become spoken comments," and by the tenor and tone of the voices, he knew the impact of what he was showing was considerable. He had met with success!

After the lights came on, the conversations of the members of the audience became quite animated. Despite their unrestrainedly favorable remarks, no one approached the photographer until the Tsar and Tsaritsa came with their children to express their appreciation. The Tsar shook hands with him once more and again reminded the photographer to contact the Minister of Transportation. At midnight, when the royal family left, Prokudin-Gorskii was surrounded by members of the Imperial Court, who proffered lavish praise and congratulations.

Particularly pleased with the outcome of the presentation was Prince M. S. Putiatin, a major-general serving as a staff officer on special duty to the Ministry of the Imperial Court. Beaming, he told Prokudin-Gorskii that he initially had high hopes for the evening and that his every expectation had not only been met but surpassed. An intimate of the Empress Alexandra, Putiatin confided that he would have full and detailed information as to the ideas of the Tsar and Tsaritsa. He proved to be a valuable and reliable conduit for Prokudin-Gorskii.

After staying the night at Tsarskoe Selo, Prokudin-Gorskii left early the next morning. Upon his arrival at his shop at 22 Bolshaia Podiacheskiia, he uncrated his equipment and immediately began to assess the needs and requirements of a full-scale expedition as outlined in his conversation with the Tsar the evening before. After assembling his data, he was ready to approach the Minister of Ways and Communications.

S. V. Rukhlov was a conscientious but mediocre bureaucrat with a balance-sheet mentality. His view of education was less idealistic than Prokudin-Gorskii's—he did not trust the public, and he viewed any demand for change as a desire to upset the existing order. But he shrewdly recognized the value of Prokudin-Gorskii's project for his own ministry, if it was properly directed. The photographer left the interview with "no doubts that the outcome would be good."

The answer was another invitation to Tsarskoe Selo. At a private audience Nicholas II outlined his requirements for pictures. The first priorities would be the photographing of the Mariinsky Canal System, as well as the old monuments of the period of Peter the Great. The Tsar appreciated the fact that Prokudin-Gorskii was accepting the Imperial commission, and he looked forward to seeing the results of the photographer's travels.

During the entire interview, nothing was said about financial matters.

*The Tsar did not say anything, because I did not ask about anything...
and the Minister did not say anything because the Tsar did not say
anything.*

Prokudin-Gorskii was certain, however, that the Tsar, having given his
consent to the project, would ensure that his needs were met.

There was in fact no need to worry about finances. Nicholas II, in the
grand Romanov manner, gave the project blanket approval and left the
details to his ministers. Rukhlov, with his fine sense of detail, made sure
that the Russian Imperial government underwrote all expenses for
mounting the expedition and provided everything necessary for the work.

In addition Prokudin-Gorskii was given two documents that he was to
keep in his pocket at all times. The first was an Imperial rescript stating
that he had the Emperor's personal permission to go "to any place in the
Russian Empire—whether secret or not." The second, a *prikaz*, or order,
furnished by the minister, stated that the Tsar considered Prokudin-
Gorskii's mission to be of such importance that all officials should render
whatever aid was necessary for the successful completion of the project—
"at any place, at any time."

To take him on his travels, Prokudin-Gorskii received "a Pullman coach
which had been specially modified for [his] use." It boasted a completely
outfitted laboratory, including a darkroom, so that processing could be
done en route. Included were quarters for Prokudin-Gorskii and his
assistants, one of them being his twenty-year-old son, Dmitri. There were
amenities such as hot and cold running water and ice. The entire coach was
Prokudin-Gorskii's domain, to use as he saw fit. "Attached to his service"
was a guide who was to help the photographer with the problems of
routing, scheduling, and logistics.

Because he was to traverse the Mariinsky System, a special ship from the
Ministry of Ways and Transportation was put at his disposal, which was
"more or less suited for his work." There was also a smaller ship available
for those waterways requiring a vessel of shallow draft. A motor launch
was used whenever the larger vessels were inconvenient.

The first assignment was "completed in July 1909." When Prokudin-
Gorskii showed the slides to Rukhlov, he made sure that all the latter's
requested subjects (aids to navigation, lifesaving stations, bridges, dams,
locks, and so on) were prominently displayed. Well-satisfied with the
subject matter, Rukhlov arranged for another invitation to be sent from
Tsarskoe Selo.

As Prokudin-Gorskii had perceived, Nicholas II was not at all interested
in the mundane and trivial shots of semaphore signals and depth markers,
so the preponderance of the photos chosen for the second evening at the
palace dealt with those things for which Nicholas had expressed a special
love—the monuments and the churches that represented the old Russia, and

Prokudin-Gorskii (right, foreground)
on the Trans-Siberian railway

the natural wonders of the empire. The Tsar inquired as to whether the photographer's needs had been adequately met: Could the transportation be improved? Was there any special equipment he should have? Did he receive the cooperation necessary? Prokudin-Gorskii replied that Rukhlov had arranged everything in such a manner that he could not be more pleased. As he was leaving, the Tsar expressed a desire to follow Prokudin-Gorskii's future travels, and asked if the photographer's schedule would permit him to undertake another assignment that year. When Prokudin-Gorskii answered in the affirmative, Nicholas said: "When you are ready to go on the next assignment, please call Count Benckendorff. He will relay the message and I will set a date for an audience." Accordingly Prokudin-Gorskii, after taking care of domestic and business affairs, spent a month (August 17–September 12, 1909) photographing the Ural region.

The commission remained open-ended. The years from 1909 to 1915 passed with little change in the routine. Prokudin-Gorskii would propose an area for photographing; consult with Rukhlov as to itinerary and receive specific direction; discuss his proposed trip with Nicholas; arrange for supplies and equipment; travel for several months, taking and developing pictures; and on his return meet with Rukhlov before his formal presentation at Tsarskoe Selo.

He wrote about this period while in exile:

On the one hand, my work was very pleasant. I received ships, etc., which were of great value in my work.... on the other hand, my work was very hard because I needed a lot of knowledge and experience, and I was often working under a great deal of pressure.

The pressure was mostly due to technical factors:

What really made it difficult was the different lighting [situations]. I worked from early in the morning to late in the afternoon hours, shooting pictures of different places from several positions. To do this I had to take my equipment from place to place [often carrying it up and down hills]. I worked late into the night to see if the pictures were any good. If not, then I took them over again. After I had the appropriate pictures, I put them in the album.

In 1910 he photographed the Volga region, including Ples, Kostroma, and Yaroslavl among his stops. The next year he took pictures at Borodino and other places associated with the "Great Fatherland War" to have the slides ready for the centennial celebration of the defeat of Napoleon. Keeping in mind also the tercentenary celebration of the accession of Mikhail Romanov (1613), he photographed historical artifacts relating to the dynasty. He wanted the Tsar to have a personal pictorial document of the glorious history of Russia and the Romanovs.

During one audience with Nicholas II he returned to a subject that had come up in their original conversation. At the intermission in his presentation on Turkestan he asked the Tsar if he "could use the pictures he had taken for educational purposes, with the understanding that all places having strategic value would be omitted." The Tsar replied: "I would be very happy if the children who are the same age as my son would learn about our great motherland from your pictures." He then asked Prokudin-Gorskii to prepare an album for the Tsarevich Alexis, stating that this would be a valuable resource "for the future heir to the Russian throne."

The Tsar's reply gave Prokudin-Gorskii the sanction to work on the aspect of his project that was most important to him, but to carry out his ideas fully, he would have to reduce the cost of reproducing the slides, which at the time was prohibitively high for the scale of the project. Unfortunately his commission for the government consumed more of his time than anticipated, as did his other activities. The solution to the problem of mass production eluded him as well.

Throughout this period his laboratories and workshops continued in operation. In addition he gave over one hundred presentations of his slides at various scientific institutions and government ministries, as well as to the general public.

When the question of recognizing photographs as art—thus entitling the photographer to the right of authorship—was raised, Prokudin-Gorskii was called before a special committee of the State Council to testify. His testimony, buttressed by a dramatic demonstration using color slides, helped in securing the right of authorship for photographers under law. His own petition to the Duma in 1911, requesting that the government purchase his work for a public museum, met with no success, however.

Above left: The Tsarevich Alexis
Right: The photographer with his wife and daughter, Hélène, in Nice c. 1932–34

From 1911 onward Prokudin-Gorskii actively worked in the field of color cinematography. Maintaining his memberships in professional societies, he regularly gave addresses at conferences in Berlin, London, and Rome, and he continued his public demonstrations both inside and outside Russia.

In 1913 he demonstrated his color pictures in one of the largest theatres in Paris, with both specialists and the general public in attendance. He already had an excellent reputation in France, since he had won the Grand Prix at the International Exhibition in Paris in 1900; and his new presentation received such wide acclaim that a syndicate made a very lucrative offer to him to remain in Paris. He was unable to abandon his activities in Russia, however, and he was obligated to decline.

This whirl of activity, pleasantly punctuated for Prokudin-Gorskii and his assistants by gifts from the Tsar, continued unabated until the fateful year 1914. With the outbreak of World War I, Prokudin-Gorskii cut short his travels and voluntarily relinquished the use of his railway coach so that it might be freed for military purposes. The war came to overshadow everything else in Russia, and the photographer was commissioned by the War Ministry to work with a specially appointed committee, surveying all articles of cinematography and photography—especially those of a technical nature—that arrived from abroad. He likewise was to review all incoming films. The tedium of these activities was counterbalanced by the novelty of taking pictures of the training of aviation pilots.

The war brought a halt to more than Prokudin-Gorskii's travels. By 1917 it had so strained the bonds of society that the end came for the Romanov Dynasty. The initial successes of the Russian armies on the Eastern Front—captured by Prokudin-Gorskii in a photograph of Austrian prisoners in front of their barracks in 1914—had been replaced by devastating losses. Echoes of previous wartime defeats in the Crimean War and the Russo-Japanese War—blotted out of the memory of officialdom—rumbled ominously in the lower order of society.

The Revolution of 1917 also meant that the collection of photographs Prokudin-Gorskii had taken for the Tsar were more of a liability than a source of pride. The joy of scientific discovery had changed into fear of detection. Sensitive artistry was depreciated by the commissars. Even the very landmarks he had photographed seemed transfigured. Ekaterinburg, where Prokudin-Gorskii spent part of his first summer fulfilling his Imperial commission, was the place where the royal family ended their last summer.

A decision had to be made, and in 1918 Prokudin-Gorskii left Russia with his family, embarking upon an odyssey unlike those before. This time he was never to return to St. Petersburg.

His collection of slides remained basically intact, although he was obligated to leave behind his projector and equipment. Certain pictures and negatives were deemed to have strategic value, and were confiscated by the authorities. These for the most part were the pictures taken to satisfy

Rukhlov, and according to Prokudin-Gorskii they "had no meaning for the general public." In addition he left behind ten negatives of the Romanov royal family, about which he stated only that they were "hidden in Russia." To this day there is no evidence that they have been found. He managed to take only a photo of the Tsarevich with him.

Prokudin-Gorskii and his family spent two years in Norway before departing for England. His work continued, but at a reduced pace because of financial difficulties. During his stay in London he lectured at the Royal Photographic Society, published an article in *The British Journal of Photography* on the importance of color photography for schools "and the community in general," and patented an optical system for a motion picture camera. In an effort to test it, he traveled to Nice in 1922, and there he took advantage of his professional experience and his contacts with the brothers Lumière by opening a photographic lab with his two sons.

After Prokudin-Gorskii's death in Paris in 1943, the collection passed into the hands of Mikhail and Dmitri, who had followed their father's profession. World War II had considerably reduced their financial circumstances, and it is at this juncture that other forces intervened. In the late 1940s and early 1950s the Russian translation program of the American Council of Learned Societies translated and published about thirty Russian twentieth-century works of science and scholarship. When its funds ran out, several works were left in a semi-completed and unpublished state. Among them was the classic nine-volume *History of Russian Art,* a composite work under the general editorship of Igor Grabar.

When the question of printing the first translated volume arose, the committee directing the enterprise set about exploring the possibility of including color illustrations. The translator, Princess Marie Putiatin, recalled that at the turn of the century Putiatin, her father-in-law, had introduced to the reigning Tsar a certain Professor Prokudin-Gorskii, who had developed a method of producing color pictures by color-separation photography. She believed that the professor's sons were living in Paris as refugees and that they were in possession of his collection of slides.

Mortimer Graves, executive director of the American Council of Learned Societies, took it upon himself to contact John Marshall, the Paris representative for the Rockefeller Foundation, who located Prokudin-Gorskii's two sons. Subsequently Marshall was able to secure approximately sixteen hundred plates for the sum of $5,000 in 1948. The ACLS brought them to the attention of the Library of Congress, where they now reside in the Prints and Photographs Division.

Village Life

*I went through the village and looked into windows. Poverty and ignorance
were everywhere, and I reflected on the slavery of earlier days. Formerly, the cause was
visible, and the chain which bound the peasants easily perceived. Now there
is no chain....With us one can still see the ropes...that still hold down that giant,
the people, so firmly that it cannot move.*

—Tolstoy

The timelessness of life in the Russian village gave it a picturesque quality, but for the Russian peasant the realities of existence were harsh. The poverty-stricken village was a permanent fixture of the Russian countryside and stood out in sharp contrast to the splendors of Tsarskoe Selo.

After Russia's defeat in the Crimean War, Alexander II had announced his intent to abolish serfdom—a measure long overdue. With the growth of industrialization in Europe, Russia could no longer afford the inefficiencies perpetuated by the system of human bondage. The economic arguments were reinforced by the very real dangers of peasant rebellion.

But although Alexander's Emancipation Manifesto of March 3, 1861, freed the serfs from personal bondage, it did not result in any widespread improvement of their social condition. In most cases the government paternalistically transferred the land to the peasant commune (the *mir*). As each household was responsible to the *mir*, so too was each individual responsible to the household—including joint responsibility for taxes and redemption dues.

By the turn of the century the problem of peasant overpopulation, coupled with the shortage of land, brought despair and anger to the countryside. A major restructuring effort that would permit private ownership of land was necessary, but it would not come until the Revolution of 1905 startled Nicholas II into allowing the dissolution of the *mir*. It was hoped that this "wager on the strong"—would stimulate a demographic shift to the towns, thereby giving Russian industry the work force it so badly needed.

The village scenes photographed by Prokudin-Gorskii were taken from life, with the exception of the one rather theatrical pose in front of an *izba*, or log cabin. Perhaps the apparent tranquillity the photographer depicted allowed the Tsar to lose himself in the beauty of the "natural colors," all the time reminding himself that this—the "real Russia" that Rasputin assured him truly loved him—was loyal to the Romanovs.

Overleaf: The village of Paltoga

Left: Peasants enjoying balalaika music
Top right: A street in Korobovo
Bottom right: The village of Tokarevka

Left: In Paltoga
Above, top: The school at the
sawmill in Devyatiny
Bottom: Thatched-roof cottages,
Nikolayevka

Above: A house in Zavarino
Right: Church in Korobovo
exemplifying the town character
Below: An Olonets peasant woman in
traditional costume

Left: A peasant girl in Little Russia
(the Ukraine)
Above: A Gruzinian woman from the
Caucasus in holiday finery

The peasants of Korobovo

Women's work: *above*, cooking; *below*, breaking flax in Perm *guberniia*; and, *right*, spinning in the village of Izvedovo

Above: Karelian types, vicinity of Petrozavodsk
Right: Peasant women washing clothes

Left: The shanty of the settler Artemis
Below, *top:* Windmills that rotate on
their bases to follow the wind
Bottom: Peasants at a pond

Below: Working in the hayfield
Right: Operating a hay press, or baler

Left: Making hay at Volkhovo
Above: Peasants making hay
Below: End of a harvest: a field near
Polotsk

Top left: Frosted trees near Turovo; *bottom left:* two girls from the same village; and not far away, *below,* a frozen haystack

Vyazovaya, near the Samara-
Zlatoust Railroad

Tolstoy in his study

Tolstoy and Yasnaya Polyana

The only existing color portrait of Count Lev Nikolaevich Tolstoy (1828–1910) was taken by Prokudin-Gorskii during his two-day stay (May 22–23, 1908) at the writer's ancestral birthplace and residence, Yasnaya Polyana. For this purpose the photographer was specifically commissioned by the journal *Notes of the Imperial Russian Technological Society*.

referred to him as Russia's "evil genius." But neither Tsarist censorship of his writings nor his excommunication by the Orthodox Church in 1901 could diminish the impact of his ideas. Like a patriarch of the Old Testament, Tolstoy denounced the corruption and injustice of his age in thundering terms. In the words of historian Ivar Spector, "He was the only author in Russian literature who could speak with authority even to his rulers, who could prophesy their downfall, and yet emerge unscathed."

When he arrived, Prokudin-Gorskii must have found a rather reluctant subject who gave grudgingly of his time and paid scant attention to the procedure at hand.

Valentin Bulgakov, Tolstoy's personal secretary, noted that Tolstoy had an intense dislike for having his picture taken, and that usually "it was an extremely painful procedure." The only reason Tolstoy would even consider such an undertaking was to maintain the harmony of the household. His wife, Sofya Andreyevna, unable to accept his philosophical views, was obsessed with the need to preserve the family fortune, which Tolstoy talked of giving to the peasants. She would therefore arrange for portraits for special occasions, such as a new edition of his works, and would prevail upon Lev Nikolaevich—as he democratically insisted that everyone call him—to pose for these pictures.

Prokudin-Gorskii came to Yasnaya Polyana at a time when Tolstoyan philosophy was one of the most pervasive influences of the age. Even Nicholas II paid the great writer tribute when he

In Prokudin-Gorskii's portraits we see Tolstoy seated in the shade of the trees, and in his study, looking very much the old Russian *barin*, the grand seigneur, beneath his peasant's beard and his loose-fitting blouse; traces of the aristocratic military officer of the Crimean War are still there in the visionary pacifist. The study, with its clutter seemingly arranged in random fashion, is suggestive of Tolstoy's creative powers.

Prokudin-Gorskii's group photograph of the children at Yasnaya Polyana is an eloquent symbol of Tolstoy's ideal of a simple life close to nature. As early as 1849 Tolstoy established a school for the peasant children of his estate; in later years he wrote many of the works they used in the classroom. In essence, Prokudin-Gorskii's idea of using color in pictures as a learning device was close in spirit to Tolstoy's method of painting word pictures for his young students.

He is like a god, not a Sabaoth or Olympian,
but the kind of Russian god who "sits on a maple throne under a
golden lime tree," not very majestic, but perhaps more
cunning than all other gods.

Maxim Gorkii

When Russia had tasted lack of justice,
seeking for her sorrows' source
like the understanding of a ripened awareness,
came Tolstoy, pityingly harsh,
but with his hands tucked into his belt.

Yevgenii Yevtushenko

"And so I have reached old age, that inner spiritual
condition in which nothing of the outer world has any interest, in which there
are no desires and one sees nothing but death ahead of one."

Tolstoy, letter to N. N. Strakhov

Above: Tolstoy's study
Below: Mme. Tolstoy in her garden

Rivers and Waterways

It was only fitting that Prokudin-Gorskii should go to the village of Volgoverkhovye to photograph the source of the Volga. To the Russians, the Volga is *matushka*—"Little Mother"—a diminutive that expresses their love and affection for the mightiest river in Europe. It flows through the Russian heartland for nearly 2,500 miles and, with its tributaries, drains an area of one million square miles. Flowing slowly from the low-lying Valdai Hills, it falls only 650 feet from its source to the broad delta at its mouth and meanders and twists in a broad majestic path until it reaches the Caspian Sea. Navigable for almost its entire length, it provides Russia with one of its main links in the system of water communications.

In Prokudin-Gorskii's day, the confluence of the Volga and Oka rivers at Nizhny-Novgorod was the crossroads of Europe and Asia, and it provided the focus of commercial and military activities. Central Russia, the Urals, and Siberia beyond, as well as the Transcaucasian region, were all penetrated from here.

The historic Baltic-Volga trade route—in use since the ninth century—was formed by a series of navigable rivers and lakes that were connected by short portages. After the establishment of St. Petersburg, construction began on a series of canals to provide connections between these waterways. Called the Mariinsky Canal System, it had a total length of approximately 740 miles and allowed barges and small vessels to take goods from St. Petersburg to the Volga and on to the Caspian Sea. The photographing of this important commercial and military link was Prokudin-Gorskii's first assignment from the Tsar's Minister of Ways and Communications.

Overleaf: Bridge across the Volga, at Rzhev

Left: On the River Svir
Above: Sawyers on the Svir
Below: An Olonets native in Vytegra

Left: Flat-bottomed canal boat
Bottom left: The supervisor of the Chernyakhovsk lock gates, Pinkhus Karlinsky, at age eighty-four, after sixty-six years of service
Below: The crew of the steamer *Sheksna*
Overleaf: Fire alarm on the steamer *Sheksna*

Preceding pages: Monument to Tsar Alexander II, commemorating the completion of the Mariinsky canal system
Left: Construction of a railroad bridge across the Tobol River
Above: Signal mast at the entrance to the Sigovets Rapids
Below: Removal of the stake (needle) from a dam in the Poire system

Left: The drawbridge at Volkhov
Above: Railroad and footbridge over the River Onda at Soroka
Below: Railroad bridge across the Shuya

Left: Bank reinforcements at
Kovzha
Top right: Barrack of the
Ministry of Communications
on the River Oka
Bottom right: Fishing settlement
at Soroka

Left: Waterway near Ostrechiny
Above, top: Fishing settlement on Lake
Seliger
Bottom: The Kovzha Dam

Nets drying on Lake Seliger

Churches and Ikons

Whether it was the ikons of Andrei Rubylov (1370–1430), considered by many to be the greatest of Russian ikonographers, or the entrance gate to the monastery at Malo-Yaroslavets, "smashed by French bullets," the pictures taken by Prokudin-Gorskii showed that from the time of the conversion of Prince Vladimir of Kiev to Christianity in 988, the history of Russia was bound up inextricably with developments in the church. The religion adopted by Vladimir, the Greek Orthodox faith of the Byzantine capital, Constantinople, left an indelible mark upon Russia, and a particularly vibrant artistic heritage.

Bedazzled by the beauty and opulence of St. Sophia, set amidst the magnificence of Byzantium, the Russian princes sought to re-create these splendors in their own dominion. Kiev was soon to rival Constantinople, with its golden domes—attesting to the lavishly wrought interiors—gleaming brilliantly in the sun.

The Russian Orthodox Church spread from Kiev ("the mother of Russian cities") to Vladimir, Suzdal, Pskov, Novgorod, Tver, and eventually to Moscow. The simple Greek cross gave way to elaborate and fanciful shapes as the Russians added and modified. The onion dome, or cupola, credited to the Hansa town of Novgorod, evolved from the construction of wooden domes that could best handle the weight of the heavy northern snow. These cupolas were enhanced by tiers of massed gables (*kokoshniki*—named for a woman's headdress),

From the cathedral to the monastery, church to chapel, the devotion of the Russian people manifested itself in the Orthodox tradition. The ikonostasis—the wall of holy pictures that separated the sanctuary from the congregation—shimmered in the illumination of countless candles and oil lamps. Here the ikons of Byzantine saints (St. Basil the Great, St. John Chrysostom, St. Cyril, and warriors such as St. George and St. Dmitri) were joined by ikons of the saintly Russian hierarchy, portrayed in a manner that exchanged the austerity of the Old Testament, peculiar to Byzantium, for the warmth of the Russian art form. The Orthodox spirit of contemplation and the revelation of eternal mysteries inherent in the faith were captured by Prokudin-Gorskii's lens in all their timeless splendor. For the Tsar, a man who was sincere in his religious devotion, these photographs in particular must have projected the essence of Russia.

Left: Cathedral of SS Peter and Paul in
Lodenoye Pole
Above: The church in Vetluga, near
Zlatoust
Below: Miraculous ikon of the Digitria
Virgin, Cathedral of the Assumption,
Smolensk

Left: The main building of the Nilova
Pustyn Monastery near Svetlitsa
Below: New Church of the
Assumption in the Gethsemane
Hermitage, Nilova Pustyn Monastery

Two views of the Cathedral of St.
Nicholas in Mozhaisk, *above* and *right*
Below: The Spaso-Borodino Monastery

Left: Trinity Cathedral, Kostroma
Above: Detail of a wall of St. Nicholas Cathedral, Mozhaisk
Below: The cedar grove at the Tolgskii Monastery, where an ikon of the Tolgskii Virgin appeared

Left: At Cherdyn, the Chapel of the Savior, built over the graves of soldiers fallen in battle
Below, top: The Church of the Resurrection in the Grove, Kostroma
Bottom: Detail of Trinity Cathedral, Kostroma

Left: Church of St. John the Baptist,
Yaroslavl
Above: Detail of the Church of SS
Peter and Paul, Yaroslavl
Below: Cathedral of the Assumption,
Kostroma

The Solovetskii Monastery at Perm, near Murmansk. *Left*, the corner tower of Trinity Cathedral; *below left*, the entrance to the Cathedral; *below right*, inside the Solovetskii monastery

Left: Monks at work planting potatoes
near Svetlitsa
Above: Monastery of SS Boris and
Gleb, Torzhok

At Nyrab. *Left, top:* the tomb of the boyar Mikhail Nikitich Romanov in the winter cathedral; *bottom, below, and overleaf:* the principal church in the Goritskii Monastery

Left: Gate of the Chernoostrov
Monastery in Malo-Yaroslevets,
peppered with French bullets during
Napoleon's invasion
Above: South portal of the Cathedral
of the Transfiguration in Tver, where
the relics of St. Mikhail of Tver rested
Below: Cathedral of Minsk,
Byelorussia

Left: Church of the Transfiguration,
inside the fortress wall at Vyelozersk
Above: The 200-year-old Church of
the Assumption, Devyatiny

Left: Frescoed walls of the Cathedral
of the Assumption, Yaroslavl
Above: The entrance to the
Borisoglebskii Monastery
Below: Church of SS Clement and
Peter in New Ladoga

Above: At Petrozavodsk, a chapel dating to the time of Peter the Great
Below: Abbess Mother Taisia of the Lushino Convent, on the veranda
Right: Hermitage of the Assumption at Lushino

At the Verkhoture Monastery. *Left*,
Abbot Xenophon; *above*, the bell
tower of the ancient Church of the
Ogiditria Virgin
Below: An old church in Kannesemga

Left: Old church of the Tikhoin Virgin on the right bank of the Tvertsa
Below: Spring on Olga Hill, Goritskii Monastery

Left: Ancient waterside chapel
Above: Byrob, chapel and spring on the spot where the ikon of St. Nicholas the Miracle Worker appeared
Below: At Byelozersk, the ancient wooden church of the prophet Elias

Left: At Borzhom, the Timotis-Ubani
Monastery
Top: Chapel of Tsar Peter I near
Petrovskoye
Above: Chapel on the site where
Byelozersk was founded in ancient
times

Left, top: Chapel in Myatusov
Bottom: Unidentified portal in a monastery
Right: Chapel on Mount Blagodat at the Kushvin Works

Ancient chapel on the lake front
at Ostashkov

Below: The *kremlin* (fortress) of the Metropolitan's palace in Rostov Velikii, on the shores of Lake Nero
Right: Ancient chapel in Ostashkov

Top: At the Monastery of the
Assumption, Staritsa, a winding-
sheet embroidered by Anastasia
Romanov, wife of Ivan the Terrible,
in 1543
Above: In Ostashkov, Holy Trinity
Church in the Zhitny Monastery
Right: Church of St. John the Baptist,
Old Ladoga

Left: Church of St. John the Baptist, Old Ladoga
Above: The Dabskii Monastery, built in 1175 by the father of Queen Tamara
Below: Tablet with inscription in the Chapel of the Savior, Cherdyn

Top: Painting of the Day of Judgment, Pidma
Bottom: Ancient cross in the Convent of the Assumption, Old Ladoga
Right: At Borodino, an ikonostasis in the Borodino Church

Left: Ikonostasis in the Church of the
Transfiguration, Byelozersk
Above: Tikhvinskoi Ikon of the
Mother of God in the Church of the
Iap Ipatevskii Monastery, Kostroma
Below: Ikonostasis in the old Church
of the Tikhoin Virgin, Torzhok

In the Museum at Tver. *Top*, detail of
a candlestick; *below*, wood carvings
of the Korchevka district; *right*, the
wonder-working ikon of the
Odigitria Virgin, Church of the
Virgin, Smolensk

Below: Shrine of the revered Dmitrii of Rostov at the Spaso-Yakovlevskii Monastery
Right: Ikonostasis in the Winter Church of the Fedorovskii Mother of God

Top: Vestments of the Patriarch Job at
the Monastery of the Assumption,
Staritsa
Bottom: Column in the Church of
John the Baptist, Kostroma
Right: Ikonostasis of the Church of
Count Shermetev

The Urals

Ah, how silvery
are the rails of Ural steel!
O main line! Main line.

—Yevgenii Yevtushenko

The Trans-Siberian Railway, over which Prokudin-Gorskii traveled from August 17 to September 12, 1909, was forged from Ural steel, and it was only fitting that he should visit that industrial region.

Located in East European Russia, the Urals, one of the world's oldest mountain ranges, stretch north to south for approximately 1,500 miles, from the Arctic Ocean to the Caspian Sea. Together with the Ural River, they form the traditional boundary between Europe and Asia, and separate the Russian plain from the western Siberian lowlands. Rich in mineral resources, the Ural area was one of the key factors in Russia's industrialization efforts, having a history that predated the achievements of Peter the Great.

It was Peter who decreed that state-supervised monopolies be set up and that the mining and metallurgical industries use serf labor to maintain their operations. Generations of serf workers, made the region the largest pig-iron producer in the world by 1800.

By the early 1900s, other industries of equal importance had arisen. The timber industry employed thousands; deposits of potassium salts, copper, and potash contributed to the needs of the growing economy; a chemical complex had been developed on the Upper Kama River; and the mining of gold and precious stones—emerald, chrysoberyl, topaz, and amethyst—allowed the Tsarist regime to maintain the brilliance of the Imperial Court and to pay its international debts.

To get to some areas that were nearly inaccessible, Prokudin-Gorskii used a Model-T Ford, as "there were no suitable vehicles made in Russia at the time." From the entrance gates at the Tagil Works (dating back to Peter the Great) to Ekaterinburg, one of the oldest metallurgical centers in the Urals, the photographer graphically portrayed Russia's industrial expansion. In viewing Prokudin-Gorskii's pictures Nicholas II could assess the advances already made and project an even greater future for Russia as she exploited the resources of these territories.

Overleaf: Workers at the Bakalsk ore mine

Above: Workers' children at play
Below: At the Kyshtym Works, dwellings for the laborers
Right: Work crew at the Satkinsk Government Factory before a pile of wood used for roasting ore

Left: The Satkinsk Government
Factory: side view of manufacture
Above: A view of the Station of
Yorezan and the Yurezan Bridge

Top left: The Martenovskaia open-hearth plant at the Kushvin Works near Mt. Blagodat (Note the date of construction under the Imperial eagle.) At the Tagil works. *Below,* entrance gates from the time of Peter the Great; *bottom left,* copper smelting furnaces of the Vyisk Works

Right: Excavation at Ketava-Ivanov
works.
Bottom left: View from the rear
platform at Simsk station

Below, top: The Kharitonov house in
Ekaterinburg
Bottom: At Perm, the Administration
Building of the Ural Railroad Lines
Right: Stone polishing at Imperial
Lapidary Works in Ekaterinburg

At Zlatoust, a view of the Zlatoust
Works, with Mount Tagonii in the
distance

Left: A general's country house in the Urals
Top: Chapel of St. Nicholas the Miracle Worker, Vetluga
Bottom: Summer quarters of the Exchange at Perm

The Kasli Works. *Left*, workshops for making artistic iron castings; *below*, the artisans busy with their molds

City of Zlatoust. *Left,* a workshop for scabbards at the Zlatoust Works; *top right,* Andrey Kalganov, former skilled worker, with his son and grandchild; *bottom right,* dwellings on a Zlatoust street

Village in the Urals

Right: A settler and his family

Top left: A Bashkir house
Left: Bashkir at his doorway
Right: Young Bashkir

The Caucasus

The rugged Caucasus Mountains, a 745-mile range extending between the Black and the Caspian seas, was long considered the boundary between Europe and Asia. Legend and history had blended together there in a way that captured the imaginations of several generations of Russians.

Corresponding to the rugged and broken character of the region was the diversity of nationalities and tribes inhabiting the pockets and valleys of the Caucasus foothills—Georgians, Abkhazians, Kurds, Laks and Chechens, Armenians, Azerbaijanians, Kalmyks, Karachais, Tatars, and Cherkessians.

Russian involvement in the Caucasus went back to the region of Paul I (1796–1801), when some tribal chieftains, caught between the rival powers of Persia and Turkey, appealed for aid. Although Russian attacks on Persia met with approval, Russian efforts to establish her suzerainty over her defenseless neighbors did not. Russian subjugation of the Caucasus met with resistance in the person of Shamil, who became the organizer of a strong nationalistic movement among the Moslem mountaineers of Daghestan. He launched a *ghazawatt* (holy war against infidels), all the while ruling his domain of narrow valleys and towering cliffs with an iron hand. The Daghestan resistance was shattered in 1859. By 1864 the Russian goal of "pacification" had been achieved.

All that remained was the peaceful exploitation of the Transcaucasian region, a policy that was implemented almost immediately. The northern region was noted for grain production, viniculture, and stock breeding, while the south had plantations that specialized in the growth of subtropical crops. Once firmly under Russian domination, the area yielded its mineral wealth in ever-increasing quantities. Alfred Nobel tapped the oil reserves of the Baku region, and by the turn of the century the region yielded nearly eighty percent of Russia's total oil production.

The forested mountain slopes with their wild grandeur provided a majestic backdrop for Prokudin-Gorskii's photos. The images of Armenians, Tatars, Gruzinians, Kurds, and Daghestans convey a sense of pride and struggle.

Overleaf: Lower Gunib, West Daghestan

Top: Daghestan man and wife
Left: Armenian women in
holiday dress
Right: Grorge Street in Artvin

Above: Nikolayevka: Gruzinian
woman in national costume
Below: Daghestan women
Right: Place of Shamyl's capture.
Shamyl (1797-1871) led the mountain
people's resistance to the Russians
until his capture in 1859.

Above: Fierce and proud, the
Daghestan tribesman proved to be a
formidable foe for the Russians.
Below: Mullah with pupils
Right: Mullahs in the mosque of
Azizy near Batum

Top left: Kurd woman with children
Bottom left: Chinese master tea grower Lau Dzhen-dzhan
Below: A group of tea gatherers—Greek women and girls

Below, top: Metekh Castle, Tiflis
Bottom: Mosque in the Asiatic
quarter of Tiflis
Right: Persian Tartars

Left: A grove at the Chakva Tea
Plantation near Batum
Above: The sorting department,
Chakva tea works, near Batum
Below: The weighing department,
Chakva tea works

A hotel at Gagry

Above: Likani Château in Borzhom, a
noted spa
Below: The Eugene spring, near
Borzhom
Right: Ugoluk dacha, or country
house, Sochi

Left: A shipment of Borzhom's
mineral water
Right: The Catherine spring, near
Borzhom

Portrait of a lady, 1910

Turkestan and Samarkand

Turkestan, the historic region of Central Asia, was the bridge between East and West. The exotic quality of Bukhara, Tashkent, and Samarkand, the major cities of this region, obviously captured Prokudin-Gorskii's imagination. Samarkand— had been a legend for centuries. As the photographer approached the public square called the Registan ("sandy place") in the center of the ancient city, imposing buildings faced with blue-green tiles shimmered before his eyes, summoning up the magic of the past.

The exact date of Samarkand's founding is not known, but legend places it some 5,000 years ago in the reign of King Aphrasiab. The first written reference to Samarkand came in a description of Alexander the Great's campaign of 329. Although Alexander was impressed with the beauty of the town, he had it destroyed because of the resistance of its inhabitants.

Recovery took some time, but eventually prosperity returned under the Kushan empire. By the seventh century A.D. Samarkand was controlled by local rulers and had gained great repute as camel caravans traveled with their loads of silk along the Tashkent Road. Chinese sources show that it was an important center for trade and commerce, specializing in chain mail, ornaments, and pottery.

It was under Timur Leng (Tamerlane) in the fourteenth century that Samarkand reached its greatest splendor. The Tatar conqueror embarked upon an extensive building program. The ancient town walls were restored, sumptuous palaces were built, gardens were laid out, and the Great Mosque Bibi Khanum was erected (1399–1404).

By the end of the seventeenth century Samarkand's fortunes had declined considerably from the days of medieval splendor when the city had been a wonderland of palaces, with tree-lined streets and an elaborate water system. Internecine wars among the Uzbek aristocracy and the devastation of the countryside by nomadic tribes had depopulated it. In the 1770's, after a fierce struggle with Russian troops, the Emir of Bukhara signed a treaty by which Samarkand was annexed to Russian Turkestan.

In the early 1900's, there was much interest in Samarkand among Russian oriental scholars. Prokudin-Gorskii provided Tsar Nicholas II with a detailed and graphic view of this exquisite jewel in his Imperial crown.

Overleaf: Tillia Kari on Samarkand's Registan Square

Below left: Nazar Magomet, a
Turkish priest/official
Right, top: Camels near the
Saliuktinskii Mines
Bottom: Kirghiz husband and
wife in front of their yurt

Left: Caravan driver and camel at rest
Below, top: Kirghiz nomads
Bottom: A nomad woman stands before her yurt.

Left: Kneeling for prayers in a mosque
Above: Palace of the Emir, in the old city of Bukhara
Below: A mosque at Shah Zindeh, on the outskirts of Samarkand, a remarkable complex of tombs and mosques built between the thirteenth and fifteenth centuries

Left: Two mullahs at Shah Zindeh mausoleums near Samarkand
Above: A clerk in Bukhara
Below: A courtyard outside a workshop in Samarkand; the building is constructed of clay.

Above: Sentry and obsolete cannon
guard the Emir's palace.
Below: Shepherd near
Samarkand—Prokudin-Gorskii made
special note of his *chapan*
(headgear).
Right: Palace of the Emir Shir-Budun,
outside Bukhara

Above: Kush-Beggi, Minister of
Internal Affairs, Bukhara
Below: Interior of the palace of the
Emir of Bukhara
Right: Opposite facade, palace of the
Emir Shir-Budun, on the outskirts of
Bukhara (See p. 181.)
Overleaf: Sart cemetery near
Sur-Darga

Left: Sart tribesman
Above: Minaret and cupola of the
Shir-Dor *madrasah* (Muslim school)
on Samarkand's Registan Square,
built during the years 1619–36
Below: Passage of death near the
tomb of Timur the Lame
(Tamerlane), Samarkand

Above: A mullah with his Sart pupils
Below and right: Two houses of Sart
tribespeople in Samarkand

Left: The Ulugh Beg *madrasah*, Samarkand, the first public building on Registan Square, dated between 1417 and 1420
Above: A small mosque on Chapan-Ata Mountain, dating from the reign of Ulugh Beg (1409–49)
Below: One of the six city gates of ancient Samarkand

Above: A *chaikhana*, or Uzbek teahouse
Below: A shop selling *shashlyk*, or shish kebab
Right: Tillia Kari. This Moslem college, begun in 1646-47, was the last building on Registan Square erected with polychrome revetments.

Above: A fruit vendor's stand
Below: Shashlyk, or shish kebab
Right: A dry-goods merchant

Above: Fat-rumped sheep noted for
their meat and coarse fleece
Below: A policeman of Samarkand
Right: A water carrier on the city
streets

Below: Along the city's back streets
Top right: A carpenter working on a beam
Bottom right: Jewish schoolboys with rabbi

Below: On a road in Samarkand
Right: The Mosque Bibi Khanum,
hastily built, suffered severe damage
in the earthquake of 1897.

Above: Sart woman
Below: Chained prisoners; the famous anarchist Prince Peter Kropotkin described such fettering in his *In Russian and French Prisons.*
Right: The *peshtak* (main portal) of the Shah Zindeh Mosque
Overleaf: Ruins of the Mosque Bibi Khanum, erected by Tamerlane between 1399 and 1404

Above: Sart woman
Below: Chained prisoners; the famous
anarchist Prince Peter Kropotkin
described such fettering in his *In
Russian and French Prisons.*
Right: The *peshtak* (main portal) of
the Shah Zindeh Mosque
Overleaf: Ruins of the Mosque Bibi
Khanum, erected by Tamerlane
between 1399 and 1404

Below: On a road in Samarkand
Right: The Mosque Bibi Khanum,
hastily built, suffered severe damage
in the earthquake of 1897.

The inner courtyard of the
Shir-Dor *madrasah*

A gathering of native tribesmen

Afterword

PROKUDIN-GORSKII AND THE PHOTOGRAPHIC TRADITION
by Arthur Goldsmith

To record the world in color was a mimetic dream shared by Prokudin-Gorskii with those who invented the first successful method of monochromatic photography. Beaumont Newhall in his *The History of Photography* quotes from a letter written in 1827 by Joseph Niepce regarding a visit with Louis Daguerre and the attempts of his future partner to register each of the "seven primary colors" onto a light-sensitive substance. Neither Daguerre nor Niepce succeeded, but the introduction of the silver-toned Daguerreotype and the monochromatic paper-negative process simultaneously invented by William Talbot were sufficient miracles to astound the world and establish photography as a potent new form of image-making. However, the public craved color, and soon after the Daguerreotype process was made public in 1839, the hand-tinting of Daguerreotypes became popular, providing income for miniaturist portrait painters, whose profession was rapidly becoming obsolete because of the new technology.

By the time Prokudin-Gorskii began his great project of documenting the Tsarist Empire with a color camera, considerable progress had been made in directly recording color by photographic means. Prokudin-Gorskii's technique was a modification of the "additive" approach to color photography, the practicality of which was first demonstrated by the physicist James Clerk Maxwell and the photographer Thomas Sutton in 1859. Maxwell believed that the impression of all colors of the spectrum, including white, could be created by adding (hence "additive") three primary colors: red, blue, and green. (The additive theory applies only to transmitted light, not to the mixing of opaque pigments.)

For the demonstration, a multicolored tartan ribbon was used. Sutton photographed the ribbon four times, once through a glass cell containing a solution of blue liquid, once through green, once through red, and once through yellow. (The reason Maxwell added a yellow exposure is not clear. It was not necessary, since the mixture of red and green light produces yellow.) Positive glass-plate images were printed from each of the resulting black-and-white negatives. The image photographed through the blue medium was illuminated by blue light, the "green" image by green light, the "red" by red light, and the "yellow" by yellow light. When simultaneously projected to form a single overlapping image, "a sort of photograph of the striped ribbon was produced in the natural color."

Prokudin-Gorskii's crucial demonstration at Tsarskoe Selo Palace more than thirty years later, which so entranced Tsar Nicholas and his court, was a more sophisticated application of a similar principle, executed with commendable showmanship.

Prokudin-Gorskii used a camera that produced three individual color-separation negatives with one loading. Apparently the opening and closing of the shutter, the changing of the three color filters, and the shifting of the glass plate to position it for the three exposures were effected automatically by a spring-powered mechanism. To achieve exact registration with a one-second interval or so between exposures, the camera had to be securely mounted and the photographer was limited to non-moving subjects. Although most of Prokudin-Gorskii's surviving work is scenic and architectural, he also made a number of portraits and charming genre studies. In historical perspective, a three-second exposure is not excessive for a posed subject; many great portraits up to the introduction of fast-dry plates in the 1880s required exposures of several seconds' duration. However, some of the photographs reproduced in this book would seem almost impossible to achieve by a succession of exposures; for example, the two prisoners chained together (page 202).

The limitation of Prokudin-Gorskii's device was solved by the invention of the "one-shot" color camera, which simultaneously made three color-separation exposures by means of a beam-splitting prism. Prokudin-Gorskii later patented such devices himself, including a cinematographic color camera. Is it possible he used an early model one-shot camera for some of his pre–World War I photographs? Pending discovery of further information, we do not know.

One-shot color cameras were widely used for commercial photography up to about the time of World War II and continue to play a role in graphic arts technology today. However, the future of color lay in other directions. Methods of obtaining photographic images in full color directly on film with one exposure were being used with considerable success by the turn of the century, and innovative pioneer though he was, Prokudin-Gorskii's efforts were mostly directed to a branch of color photography doomed to become obsolete.

By 1903 in France, the Lumière brothers (Louis and Auguste) had developed their autochrome method of making positive color transparencies for viewing or projecting. Autochromes were placed on the market in 1907 and soon were being used by a number of distinguished photographers including Arnold Genthe, Frank Eugene, Alfred Stieglitz, and Edward Steichen. The autochrome plate was coated with a random mixture of tiny grains of starch dyed red, green, and blue, which acted as a built-in color-separation screen over which a light-sensitive emulsion was coated. The exposure was made through the back of the plate. The resulting negative was transformed into a positive image, resulting in a transparency that created the colors of the subject. The image was grainy, softly defined, and subdued in color saturation, but possessed a pictorial charm prized by artist-craftsmen of the time and appreciated today. During the 1920s, Prokudin-Gorskii paid tribute to the advantages of the autochrome, analyzed its limitations, and with prophetic insight predicted it would be supplanted in the near future by "fresh steps...leaving behind all existing methods." The fresh steps, in the event, involved color dyes in subtractive

primary colors (cyan, magenta, and yellow), which led to the invention of Kodachrome and the wide range of color-print and transparency films of today.

Color prints could be made from Prokudin-Gorskii's separation negatives, but it was a laborious and expensive process. The most effective way to show the images was by projection, for which purpose the photographer designed his own equipment. Three precisely formed rhomboidal prisms were cemented together in such a way that all three color-separation slides could be projected simultaneously in sharp focus and exact register. The results, for the time, must have been impressive, as witness the enthusiastic response of the Tsar and his Court, and of the general public not only in Russia but also in sophisticated Paris.

As a photographic technician, teacher, and inventor, Prokudin-Gorskii played an important role in introducing advanced aspects of photographic technology to turn-of-the-century Russia, where strenuous, if sometimes erratic, attempts were being made to catch up with western science and industry. Since the time of Peter the Great, the westernization of Russia often was forced on a massively conservative society from the top, and it is characteristic that Prokudin-Gorskii's patron should have been the Tsar himself. As the text amply illustrates, the limitations upon Prokudin-Gorskii's freedom as an artist and documentarian were under the dictates of the Emperor and his bureaucrats. In the West, however, photographers commissioned by businessmen to glamorize the railroads or other commercial subjects also labored under certain restrictions.

Prokudin-Gorskii's deep commitment to the value of photography in education and his grand vision in attempting to photograph in color the vast Russian Empire—the most ambitious project of its type we know of—deserve recognition beyond his technical achievements. The former he held for the rest of his life, publishing an extraordinary statement on the "Importance of Colour Photography for Schools and the Community in General," in *The British Journal of Photography,* April 8, 1922, in which he promotes his contributions to color photography, attacks the triviality of contemporary cinema, and predicts the importance of visual representations as an educational aid. As for his major project, considering its scope, the limitations of his technology, and the restrictions imposed by an absolutist and sometimes paranoid regime, it was an impossible self-assignment. The remarkable extent to which he succeeded, as reflected in the photographs reproduced here, is a tribute to his skill, energy, and resourcefulness.

The color reproductions in this book were made directly from black-and-white contact prints of the original glass-plate negatives. (In some cases the emulsion had begun to peel away, accounting for occasional streaks of unnatural color noticeable at the edges of some of the reproductions.) The three black-and-white prints constituted "pre-separated" copy, which had to be translated into screened color separations for printing: yellow, red (actually magenta), and blue-green (actually cyan), plus black. This required manipulation for registration is due to the delay between each of the three exposures from color to color. Once the correct matching was established, further manipulation was required to bring all three colors into proper balance. The problem of supplying a fourth, black separation, necessary for giving the printed image adequate depth, was solved by using the "blue" or "red" exposure for this purpose. The final separations with a 150-line screen were made by laser scanning. Do the colors here accurately represent Prokudin-Gorskii's results? There is no way of telling. However, their soft, impressionistic glow is evocative of the bygone era Prokudin-Gorskii recorded, and one suspects he would be pleased.

Like many of the great topographical photographers of the American West, Prokudin-Gorskii frequently depended upon the railroad to accomplish his work, and for a similar reason: the enormous distances involved. His lavishly equipped rolling darkroom was a novelty in Russia but had prototypes in the wet-plate era after the American Civil War, when railroads were pushing west at the rate of ten miles per day and railroad companies wanted photographs to publicize their routes and achievements. We do not have a detailed log of all the miles Prokudin-Gorskii traveled, but it must have been many tens of thousands, most of it by rail.

The images that have survived, to emerge from limbo into public availability some seventy years later, are a magical glimpse into a world that is forever gone, as remote to us now as the Middle Ages, of which indeed the last days of the Tsarist empire were a lingering remnant. As an historical record, in color, they attest to the imagination and enterprise of the photographer who compiled them, reminding one of Mathew Brady's imaginative scope in deciding to document the Civil War. However, this is the work of one man, not a talented team, and the photographs were made to satisfy the needs of reactionary officials like Rukhlov, to please the capricious Tsar, and—he hoped—to edify the youth of Russia. It would not have been possible even if Prokudin-Gorskii had been so inclined, and we have no reason to believe that this was the case, to document the poverty, degradation, and cruelty of Imperial Russia as it approached the end.

Photography's potentially powerful role in documenting social, political, and economic evils was only beginning to be appreciated and utilized even in the most liberal western states during the first two decades of the twentieth century. We should not look for Jacob Riis, Lewis Hines, or Dorothea Lange here. What we have reproduced, in gentle colors as nostalgic as a half-forgotten dream, is the beautiful surface of Imperial Russia during the last days of the Tsar: its valleys, rivers, hamlets, churches, country villages, farms, and peasants, a Russian Easter Egg fantasy rendered poignant by the knowledge of how abruptly, violently, and totally it all would be smashed.

SELECTED BIBLIOGRAPHY

Alpatov, M. W. *Art Treasures of Russia*. New York, Abrams, 1967.

Billington, James H. *The Ikon and the Axe: An Interpretive History of Russian Culture*, New York, Knopf, 1966.

Bulgakov, Valentin. *The Last Year of Leo Tolstoy*, trans. Ann Dunnigan and introduction by George Steiner. New York: Dial Press, 1971.

Engel, S. "Iubileinii portret." *Ogonek*, No. 37 (September, 1978), 15.

Faensen, Hubert, Ivanov, Vladimir, and Beyer, Klaus G. *Early Russian Architecture*. New York: Putnam, 1975.

Fotograf-Liubitel'. Vols. XVI-XIX. St. Petersburg, 1905–1908.

"The Gorsky Camera for Colour Photogaphy." *The British Journal of Photography Monthly Supplement on Colour Photography*, Vol. XVI, No. 192 (November 3, 1922), 42–43.

"The Gorsky Process of Colour Cinematography." *The British Journal of Photography Monthly Supplement on Colour Photography*, Vol. XVI, No. 182 (January 6, 1922), 4.

Gurko, V. I. *Features and Figures of the Past: Government and Opinion in the Reign of Nicholas II*, Wallace Sterling, Xenia Joukoff Eudin, H. H. Fisher and trans. Laura Matveev. New York: Russell, 1970.

McDowell, Bart. *Journey Across Russia: The Soviet Union Today*, photographed by Dean Conger. Washington, D.C., National Geographic Society, 1977.

Pares, Bernard. *The Fall of the Russian Monarchy: A Study of the Evidence*. London: J. Carpe, 1939.

"Prism Lens System for Three Colour Cameras—No. 185161." *The British Journal of Photography*, Vol. LXIX, No. 3261 (November 3, 1922), 666.

Procoudine Gorsky, S. de (ed.) *Journal de la Société Photochimie ELKA*. Nice, 1926.

Prokudin-Gorskii, S. M. *Fototeknicheskoe delo: kratkii ukazatel' dlia izdatelei, redaktorov', khudozhnikov', typografii, i.t.d.* St. Petersburg, 1905.

———. "Importance of Colour Photography for Schools and the Community in General." *The British Journal of Photography Monthly Supplement on Colour Photography*, Vol. XIII, No. 161 (April 2, 1920), 13–15; Vol. XIII, No. 162 (May 7, 1920), 19–20.

———. *O fotografirovanii momental'nimi ruchnimi kamerami*. St. Petersburg, 1898.

———. *O pechatanii (kopirovanii) s' negativov'*. St. Petersburg, 1898.

———. *Russko-Iaponskaia voina, 1904–1905*. St. Petersburg, 1905.

———. Unpublished miscellaneous writings, 1920–1940 (manuscripts).

Robinson, Geroid Tanquary. *Rural Russia Under the Old Regime: A History of the Landlord-Peasant World and a Prologue to the Peasant Revolution of 1917*. Los Angeles: University of California Press, 1967.

Spector, Ivar. *An Introduction to Russian History and Culture*. 5th edition. Princeton, N.J.: D. Van Nostrand Company, Inc., 1969.

Tolstoi, Lev Nikolaevich. *Tolstoy's Letters*, ed. and trans. R. F. Christian. 2 vols. New York: Scribner's, 1978.

Tsapenko, M. *Russian Architecture (11th–17th c.)*. Moscow, no date.

Umnyakov, I., and Aleskerov, Y. *Samarkand: A Guide Book*. Moscow, 1972.

Vanderbilt, Paul. *Guide to the Special Collections of Prints and Photographs in the Library of Congress*.

Voyce, Arthur. *The Art and Architecture of Medieval Russia*. Norman, Oklahoma, University of Oklahoma Press, 1967.

Wallace, Donald Mackenzie. *Russia on the Eve of War and Revolution*, ed. and introduced by Cyril E. Black. New York: Viking, 1961.